FEAR-LESS
DO MORE

21 Amazing Ways to Create A Legacy with Flair

BY RYAN BLAIR-SMITH

To:_____

From:_____

"Too many of us are not living our DREAMS because we are living our fears."
-Les Brown

Copyright © 2017 by Ryan Blair-Smith

This book is available at quantity discounts for bulk purchases.

All rights reserved. No part of this book may be reproduced or transmitted in any form or by and means, electronic or mechanical, including photocopying, recording, or any information storage and retrieval system, without written permission from Ryan Blair-Smith except for brief quotations used in reviews, written specifically for inclusion in newspapers, blogs, or magazines.

ISBN: 978-0-9992222-0-1

Printed in the United States of America

DEDICATION

This book is dedicated in love to my mother Vernetta Peoples-Blair, my angel on earth who first believed in me before I ever believed in myself.

I also dedicate this book to my beautiful, bold, brilliant daughters Little Miss Blair Flair and Little Miss Taylor Made. May you two always know the POWER of your GREATNESS resides on the other side of fear. Thank you both for pushing me past my fears to be a better mother and woman. I am forever in love and grateful for you two!

TABLE OF CONTENTS

	The Beginning	1
Day 1	Do More	4
Day 2	Dream More	8
Day 3	Say YES More	12
Day 4	Rise More	16
Day 5	Leap More	20
Day 6	Smile More	24
Day 7	Believe More	28
Day 8	Ask More	32
Day 9	Relax More	36
Day 10	Pray More	40

TABLE OF CONTENTS CONT.

Day 11	Visualize More	44
Day 12	Forgive More	48
Day 13	Be More Intentional	53
Day 14	Connect More	57
Day 15	Take More Action	61
Day 16	Fail More	65
Day 17	Trust God More	70
Day 18	Focus More	74
Day 19	Grow More	78
Day 20	Give More	82
Day 21	Love More	86
	Gratitude Journal	89

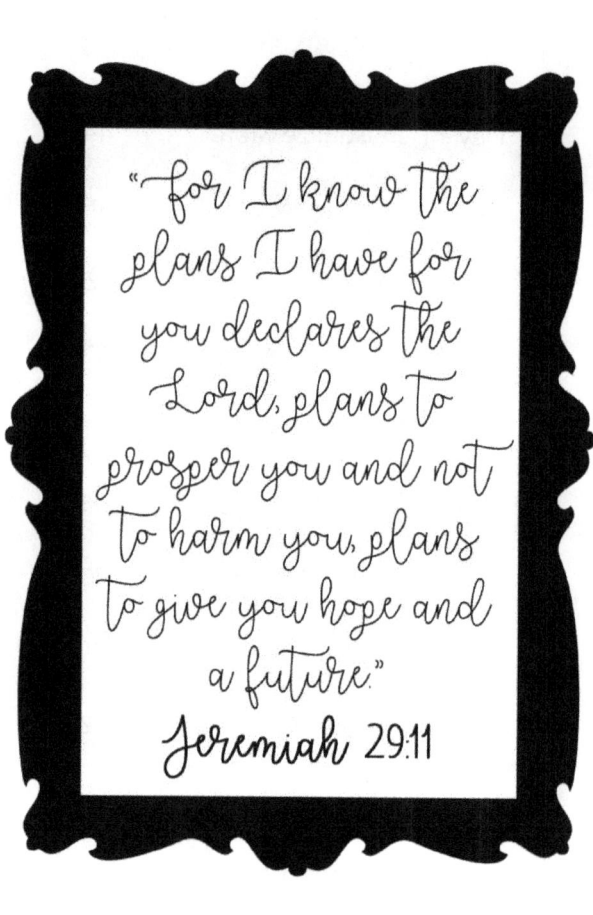

THE BEGINNING

Welcome to the 21-Day Fear-less, Do More Challenge. This challenge is designed to help you drop the fears that are keeping you from walking in your greatness. Your purpose is to let go of the fear so the real you shows up, and step over fear, so you can live your best life as Oprah says. Fearing less allows you to live a more fulfilled life. I lived way too long in the fear space in life and it did not get me closer to accomplishing anything, but grief and regret. Fear took up space where my joy was supposed to exist, flourish and grow. I pray as you journey through these 21 days with me, that you unlock some of the barriers that have kept you or are keeping you from living the life you deserve and desire. I pray you begin to live life with **F.L.A.I.R.,** where you **F**ear **L**ess and **A**ttract **I**ntentional **R**esults. I promise this quick read will be a game-changer designed to challenge, motivate, and inspire you to walk further into your destiny. Here's the secret, you were created with purpose, for a purpose, on purpose. God is up to something in your life. He needs you to push fear to the side, walk in faith, trust Him and take the first step! I pray you walk away from this book with a new outlook on what is needed from you to move to that "next" in your life. In this book, you will get a 5 to 10 minute read on the subject for the day, followed by a question and answer section to help you process what has been read. I suggest finding a quiet spot and truly taking the time to answer the questions open and honestly.

Put in action, where action is required. Let's get to work....cheers in advance!

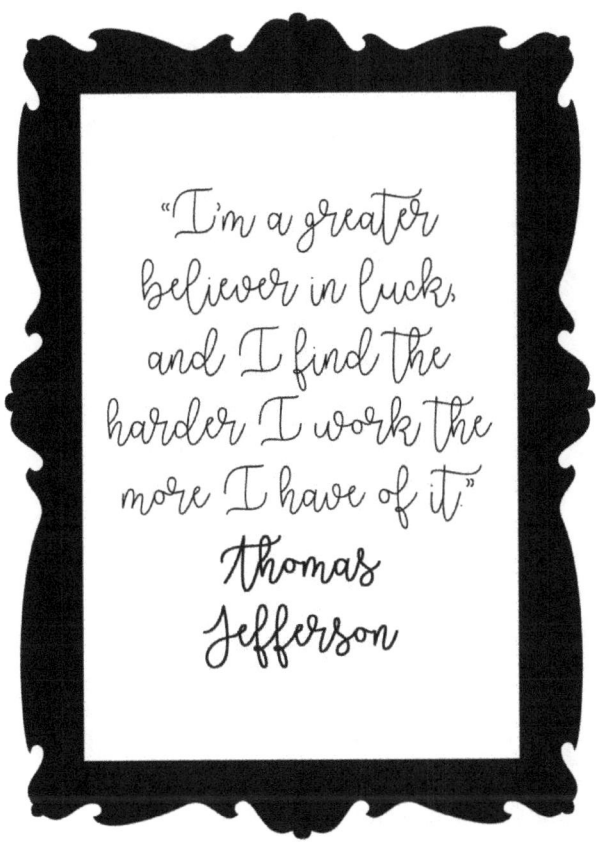

"I'm a greater believer in luck, and I find the harder I work the more I have of it."
Thomas Jefferson

DAY 1: DO MORE

"If you can't fly, then run
If you can't run, then walk
If you can't walk, then crawl but whatever you
do you have to keep moving forward."
~Martin Luther King Jr.

Welcome to day one of our 21-day adventure. I pray you walk away with more than you started with. You're reading this book, because I decided to fear less and take action. It is not easy writing a book, well finishing one, but if it is one of your desires, get to work. Pen to paper, pen to paper I tell ya! Fear-less. Do more. In order to do more, you must take action, it is as simple as that. Trapping yourself in the space of fear, will most definitely keep you from doing what you ultimately desire. In junior high school, I really wanted to play basketball. I signed up for the team, started going to practices, and guess what happened? The day we started playing actual games against other teams in front of an audience, was a wrap for me. I was fearful of playing in front of others. I froze and became too worried about what they were thinking of me. It was a crazy feeling. I stayed on the team, but was benched the majority of the time because I could not show up when it was time to be in the game. Who knows what could have happened if I would have released the fear? Heck I could have been on an WNBA squad! You're laughing, but work with me on this. Really, I could have done more!

Fear-Less Thoughts:

Think about a moment in your life where you could have done more, but froze because of fear. What was that moment?

_____
_____
_____
_____

How do you feel about it now?

_____
_____
_____
_____

What can you do today instead of fearing the unknown? List your thoughts below.

_____
_____
_____
_____
_____
_____

"Dreams often come one size too big so that we can grow into them."
John C. Maxwell

DAY 2: DREAM MORE

"The biggest adventure you can take is to live the life of your DREAMS."
~ Oprah

Close your eyes for a second and think about the last dream or vision you had. What did it look like? How did it feel to be in that space? If you could be there now, would you? Now think for a moment, have you stopped dreaming? Regardless of how you answered any of those questions; here is my response, do not stop dreaming! Dream big. Dream boldly. Dream in color. Dream so big that it scares you! While you are dreaming remember to FEAR-LESS in the process. The dreams, visions, and goals that you have been given were placed within you for a reason. It does not matter if anyone gets, or understands what was placed in you. You're the only one that needs to get it. You are the only one that can birth that dream. Here's the truth, if you continue to walk and talk in the space of fear, you will continue to push your dreams to the side or stop dreaming altogether. I do not want you to let your dreams go. I want you to dream more and do something with those dreams. Do not keep them to yourself. Do you know Les Brown a phenomenal sought after motivational speaker once said that the richest place on earth is the cemetery? Yes the cemetery. Why the cemetery? The cemetery is the richest place on earth because it is at the cemetery where all the dreams that never came to fruition are buried with those that never took a chance. I do not want you to be average, and live an average life. I want you to live a LIFE of FLAIR...where you FEAR-LESS and Attract Intentional Results.

Fear-Less Thoughts:

List a few of your dreams below, new dreams or dreams you forgot you had. Get in a quiet place and brain dump. Don't think too hard. Flow. Let me help you get started. What are your dream/goals for this year?

_____
_____
_____
_____
_____
_____
_____
_____
_____
_____

Bonus Question: When will you take action?

_____
_____
_____
_____
_____

"I refuse to be a passenger in my own life."
Crystal Layland

DAY 3: SAY YES MORE

"All you got to do is say ....YES"
~ Unknown

Say Yes!

Say yes to you. Say yes to your purpose. Say yes to your gifts. Say yes to your talents. Say yes to everything you have been saying no to. Say yes to everything you have been avoiding that encompasses who you have been designed to be. If you are feeling stuck and wondering why you are not operating at full capacity, you may need to ask yourself, have I truly said yes to me? Yes to all that God has created me to be? It's easy to say yes to others. We are quick to meet their requirements and requests. We are quick to jump on someone else's project and help them build their million or billion dollar company, but at the same time believing we are inadequate to do this for ourselves. What happens when it is time to say yes to your purpose? Yes to your standards. Yes to your capabilities. Yes to meeting the needs of your business. Yes to stepping out on faith. Yes to taking the leap in a positive direction. I challenge you once again...FEAR-Less and say YES to YOU!

Fear-Less Thoughts:

Woo.....all you have to do is SAY YASSSS! Are you saying yes to all that God is calling you to be? If no, why not? If yes, how?

_____
_____
_____
_____

What do you need to say no to, in order to say yes to you?

_____
_____
_____
_____

When's the last time you focused on you?

_____
_____
_____
_____

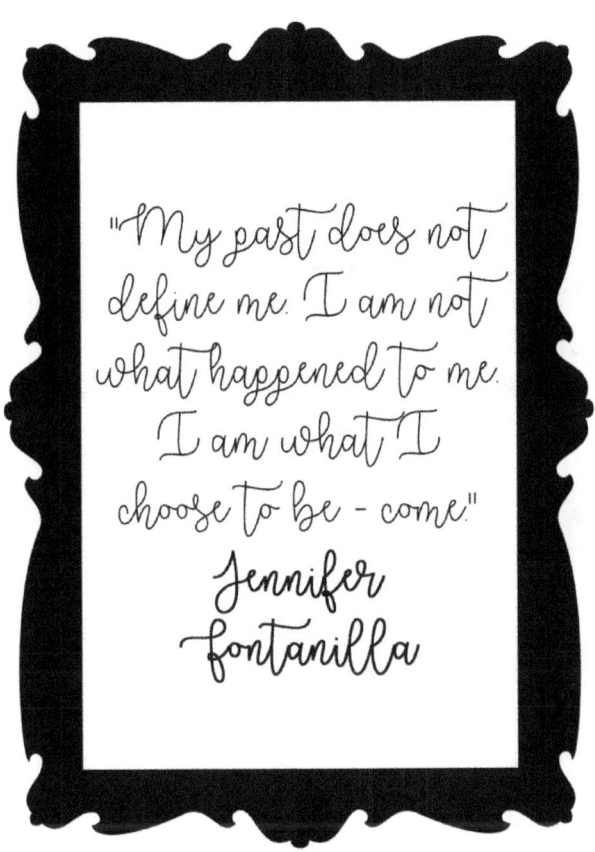

"My past does not define me. I am not what happened to me. I am what I choose to be - come."

Jennifer Fontanilla

DAY 4: RISE MORE

"Just like moons and like suns, With the certainty of tides, Just like hopes springing high, Still I'll rise."
~ **Maya Angelou**

I rise...I rise...I rise as Maya Angelou ends her poem *"Still I Rise."* I am truly fueled with a passion, desire, and sheer motivation to keep pushing towards my calling in this world. A fire ignites in me to not settle in any area of my life, to get up and rise to my full potential. Upon reading this poem, you too will be sparked to rise up from anything that is holding you back or has held you back. Sometimes in life, things can seem to make us feel as though we have hit rock bottom and recovery may seem close to impossible. I promise you, you can rise from it. You can walk away from that situation victorious with very few war wounds to remind you that you did overcome and survive. That God did have something greater for you when it seemed as though you had been counted out. I come to tell you, stop fearing the impossible. I absolutely love the song by Audra Day called *Rise Up*.

To you, I say you will rise up! You will recover, you will overcome, you will have a story to tell how you made it through, how God had more in store for you! Your story will end in victory! Take the step and rise up. Someone is waiting on your victory story so they can create their story!

Fear-Less Thoughts:

What's the story that you want to end in victory?

_____
_____
_____
_____

What is needed to rise up from?

_____
_____
_____
_____

What do you feel is currently holding you down?

_____
_____
_____
_____

When do you plan on taking steps to RISE up? (Give it a date).

_____
_____
_____
_____

DAY 5: LEAP MORE

"Leap and grow your wings on your way down."
~ Les Brown

Have you ever imagined leaping from an airplane? Wind beneath your wings? Whether you have or have not thought about the idea, let's envision this experience for a moment. As a freeing moment, a liberating moment, and a weightless experience that ends in pure bliss. It will begin as a scary moment that seems impossible to do, or even wrap your mind around. Being 12,500 feet above ground level and taking the biggest leap ever in life. On your first leap in skydiving you are always attached to a certified instructor, they call it "tandem jumps." Isn't that liberating to think about? Leaping out of that tiny plane they place you in and jumping with someone that knows the ropes that can help you through the process? They have been there and done that. I will take the assistance from an expert anytime, land safely and have something to brag about and scratch off the bucket list. Now, think about the one thing you have thought about taking a leap in your life, but have been too fearful to make it happen. Guess what? You have an expert leaping with you - God. He is right there with you and He sent you a helper to give you wisdom and protection in taking that leap. I challenge you to write that book, get on that stage, take that career change, open that new business, and simply go after that dream that has been placed within you. You have the perfect and best expert in your corner, that will catch you when you fall and place you right back on your feet. Go...leap girl....go! Cheers to you Fearing-Less and Leaping More...

Fear-Less Thoughts:

Here's the challenge and question to you....What are you currently scared of taking a leap on? Why?

_____
_____
_____
_____

When do you plan on taking that LEAP? Go...

_____
_____
_____
_____

"A smile is the best thing you can wear!"
Ryan Blair-Smith

DAY 6: SMILE MORE

"The prettiest thing you can wear is a smile."
~Unknown

Smile often. Do you know how hard it is to be mad and smile at the same time? It is darn near impossible to do. I promise it is. Try it! Research has shown that smiling is said to cause a positive effect on you. It releases stress and makes you feel happy. I don't know about you, but I would rather walk about smiling all day with joy in my heart and on my mind. They say that smiling is an attractive expression that will draw people to you rather than pass by you or push you away. You never know what a person is going through in their life and they pass by you with a bright smile and it gives them a spark, a light that they needed. It may have been a while since that stranger took time to acknowledge them with a smile and you could be that one smile they needed. I think it takes a lot of work to walk around with a frown, and let's be honest I am sure it causes some seriously bad wrinkles on your face and who wants that? I am trying to age very well and my smiling is going to help me accomplish that goal I am pretty sure. Like the quote above says..."The prettiest thing you can wear is a smile." So, today, I challenge you to FEAR-LESS and crack a smile more!

Fear-Less Thoughts:

When is the last time you smiled?

_____
_____
_____
_____

When is the last time you smiled at a complete stranger?

_____
_____
_____
_____

Find at least three to four people you can genuinely smile at today, you can even throw in a HELLO if you are feeling extra friendly. It won't hurt you. I promise! You may even meet a new friend!

_____
_____
_____
_____

FEAR-LESS DO MORE

"She turned her cant's into cans and her dreams into plans."
Unknown

DAY 7: BELIEVE MORE

*"If you believe it will work out, you'll see opportunities.
If you believe it won't, you will see obstacles."*
~Wayne Dyer

Let's start with this, "Stinkin' Thinkin" as Joyce Meyer says is a no go in your life. Your thoughts are the beginning and ending to what you will do in life. If you believe you can accomplish your dreams, chances are you will. Soon as negative thoughts, doubt, and stinkin' thinkin' creeps in, you have now sabotaged yourself from accomplishing anything. Your mindset is the number one thing that propels you forward. You must switch from thoughts of I can't, to thoughts of I can. Think about the times you had your mind made up that you were going to do something and how that situation ended. I can remember a number of times I thought about losing weight, but at the same time my mind was not fully convinced I could successfully reach my goal. In those situations I failed miserably, but the day I made up my mind that my desire to take control of my life and health was going to happen, the results came. Becoming 84lbs lighter was a victory for me and I am glad that my mind finally caught up with me believing in the possibility. A lot of times we believe we do not have the right tools, resources, strength, or other components to make things happen. In actuality, we have been given everything we need at that moment to bring our desires, dreams, and goals to pass. You have enough right now. You are more equipped than you believe. Get fear out of the way! So to you I say...FEAR-LESS and BELIEVE MORE!

Fear-Less Thoughts:

What do you need to believe more of in your life?

_____
_____
_____
_____

What negative thoughts are you telling yourself?

_____
_____
_____
_____

Write a power statement or declaration that you can post somewhere to read daily. (Example: I am called to do great things. I am bold, brilliant, and beautiful. I choose joy, happiness, and peace in my life. This year will be the most amazing year for me)!

_____
_____
_____
_____
_____
_____
_____
_____
_____
_____

DAY 8: ASK MORE

"It always seems impossible until it's done."
~Nelson Mandela

Have you ever read in the Bible James 4:2,*"You do not have because you do not ask God."* Imagine what would happen if you go to the Source, the person, the Creator of everything? If you sat and asked Him for what you wanted? And what if He answered with the blessing in question. How amazing would that be? It seems crazy that it could be that easy. Asking?! In Psalm 37:4,*"Take delight in the Lord and he will give you the desires of your heart."* Yes the desires of your heart. In life, we have opportunities to ask for things from those God places in our path, but we are scared to ask for help, guidance, or even support. We miss these moments because we allow fear to creep in and keep us stuck. Think about those times when you asked for something and you got what you desired. I challenge you to not block your blessings because of fear of asking for what you want and desire. What's the old saying? Closed mouths don't get fed. That job, that raise, that new contract, new opportunity...ask for what you want. Regardless of the answer, at least you took the step to ask. FEAR-LESS and ASK MORE!

Fear-Less Thoughts:

What is something that you have been afraid to ask for?

_____
_____
_____
_____

What are you waiting on?

_____
_____
_____
_____

When are you going to ask? (Set a date) Go get it!

_____
_____
_____
_____

"Calm is a superpower."
Unknown

DAY 9: RELAX MORE

"Protect the asset."
~ Greg McKeown

When was the last time you relaxed? Chilled out? Caught a moment of fresh air? Read a great book? When is the last time you took time for you? Sometimes, we can push ourselves so much, so far, and so hard that we forget to take a time out. Taking a moment to embrace what's going on around us versus creating what is going on around us. Appreciate being in the moment. I am currently reading *Essentialism* as recommended by my coach. It is an amazing read. There is one chapter that talks about the importance of protecting your assets, simply put taking care of yourself, getting proper sleep instead of depriving yourself of that essential time to regroup, get that brain and body recharged. In order to create amazing ideas and results in your life and business, you must get proper sleep. Sleep deprivation is a silent killer of your creative genius and well-being. Spending time to relax is not a bad thing at all and should definitely be in rotation on your calendar. So, to you I say, Fear-Less and RELAX more!

Fear-Less Thoughts:

When is the last time you took time for you?

_____
_____
_____
_____

Imagine life stress free because of you recharging. What is something you can do to incorporate relaxing?

_____
_____
_____
_____
_____
_____
_____
_____
_____
_____

"My secret is simple: I pray!"
Unknown

DAY 10: PRAY MORE

"When you pray be sure that you listen as well as talk. You have things you want to say to God but He also has things He wants to say to you."
~Joyce Meyer

The best armor you have in life is prayer! I am currently reading and studying a devotional by Priscilla Shirer, world-renowned New York Times Best-Selling Christian author and motivational speaker. The book is *The Armor of God* and it is definitely a must read. The book is based on Ephesians 6:10-20, and it talks about the armor we need to be equipped in life against an invisible war that rages around us daily and how there are actually seven pieces of armor we need to beat the enemy that rages against us. The most powerful piece in our full armor is our prayer life. When we understand that in every area of our life we need prayer to get us through, the more abundant life we live. There is power in our prayer. I was talking to a pastor and he was saying in life we are running a race, and we try to run that race with all our strength and power, it gets tough and we continue to try to tap into our strength. Really that is where we fail and why the race gets tougher because we never stop and seek God in the process. We think we got this and God is watching and waiting for us to stop and seek Him. He is literally looking at us, saying I'll wait. Knowing Him, He and the angels are giggling at us, wondering when we will stop, sit down, and get into prayer mode about our situation. In every area of our lives, we do not have to be going through anything in order to pray, we need to take time daily to communicate and hear God's will over our life to gain the strength. I challenge you to Fear-Less and Pray More. He's waiting to hear from you!!

Fear-Less Thoughts:

Question? At this very moment what do you need to stop running with on your own merit and need to sit down and pray about?

_____
_____
_____
_____

Second thing, I challenge you to get the devotional I mentioned above and get a prayer journal to write your prayers on.

_____
_____
_____
_____
_____
_____
_____
_____
_____
_____

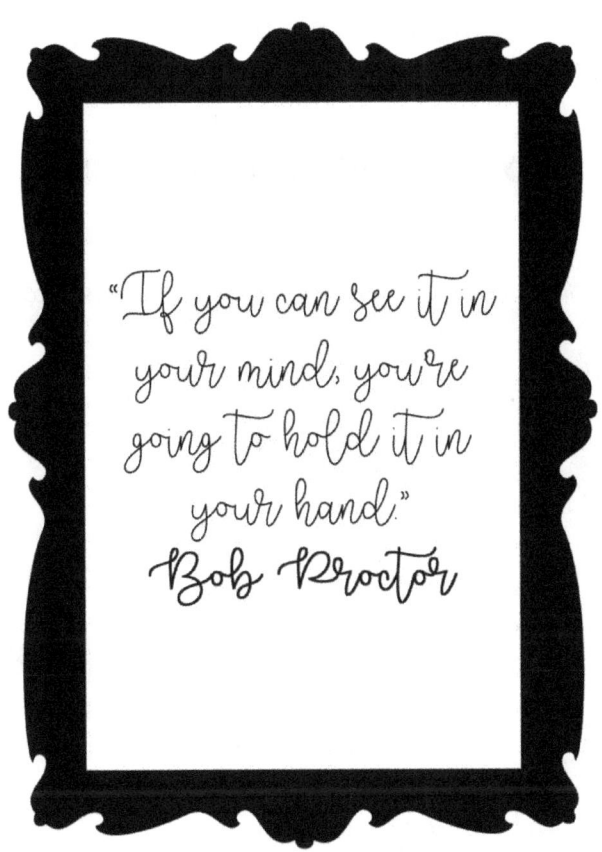

"If you can see it in your mind, you're going to hold it in your hand."
Bob Proctor

DAY 11: VISUALIZE MORE

"Vision. It reaches beyond the thing that is, into the conception of what can be. Imagination gives you the picture. Vision gives you the impulse to make the picture your own."
~**Robert Collier**

I once heard Steve Harvey say, *"If you can see IT in your mind you can hold IT in your hand."* I believe every word in that quote. The power of your vision for what you want in life can most definitely manifest itself. Having a vision for what you want is what will keep you pushing forward and seeing beyond where you currently are. You have to get that Olympic athlete tunnel vision. Where you literally see yourself crossing that finish line first, the gold medal being placed around your neck, you seeing yourself beating your best record.

Visualize it. Visualize it. Visualize it. Create the, "win before you've won" mindset. When I won the Miss Black Oklahoma State University pageant, way back when, I visualized it. I remember running in my home neighborhood and as I ran I would do this funny visualization technique that I made up, I would run and pretend I was placing a crown on my head. Work with me, I know it sounds crazy. I would visualize what I would do after getting the crown. I would visualize using my platform to inspire and motivate other women in my life. I envisioned having women workshops, seminars, and conferences that motivated, inspired, and challenged women around the world. If you're reading this, you can see that my vision has continued past those good ole college days of winning that crown. I am walking, living and breathing what I envisioned. I visualized it, I believed it, and I went for it. I walked on that stage as though I had already won. Because I could truly see the end goal. That is my challenge to you, visualize what you want, believe it, and go get it. FEAR-Less and Visualize More!

Fear-Less Thoughts:

Challenge to you, create a vision board of what you want to manifest in your life, it can be within the next six months to a year. Get a clear picture on what is next for you. You will need a foam board, magazines, scissors, glue sticks, markers, scrapbooking size cardstock in your favorite color, and glittery stickers, if that is your jam. Before you begin throwing everything you can on the board, do a brain dump on what is really important now and that you want to focus on. I would suggest on your board keeping it to two to three key things for focus. Don't forget to add favorite quotes, scriptures, affirmations, and/or power words. I am already celebrating what is about to be unleashed from you!!

_____
_____
_____
_____
_____
_____
_____
_____
_____
_____

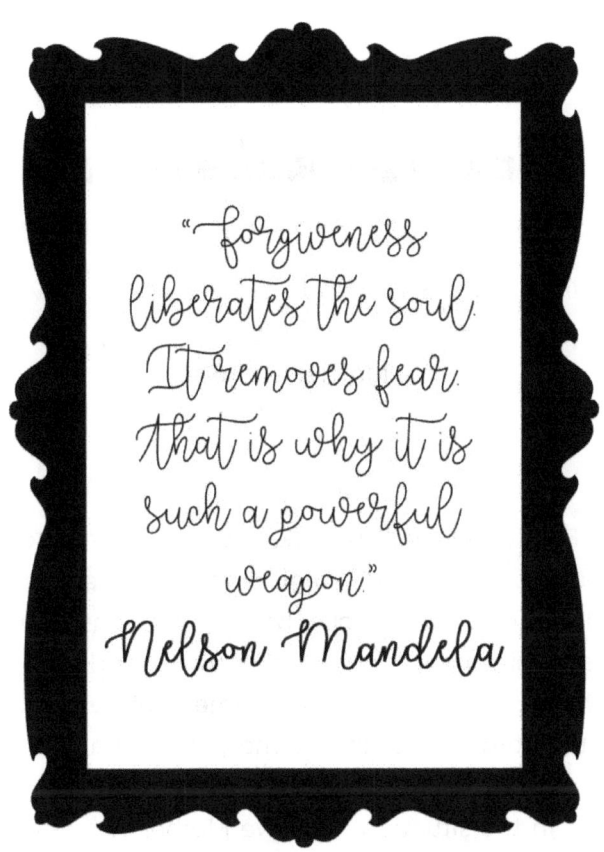

DAY 12: FORGIVE MORE

"If we really want to love we must learn how to forgive."
~**Mother Theresa**

Forgiveness will unlock doors you never knew could be unlocked. Forgiveness can break every chain that has you bound by past hurts, disappointment, mistreatment, and failed relationships. I heard many times before that the act of forgiving is not for the person that did the wrong doing, forgiving is for the person that was hurt in the situation. I believe Mother Theresa said it best, *"If we really want to love we must learn how to forgive."* Walking around with an unforgiving heart causes more problems than the actual situation. Unforgiveness will harden the heart, and corrupt the mind with vengeful thoughts. It blocks the flow of positivity, through a clear mind and heart. Simply put, it keeps you bound in a fearful state versus a freeing one. I don't know about you, but I want to stay in the positive "freeing" zone as much as possible.

If you don't mind I want to share a little deeper meaning on what **forgiving more** truly means to me. I hope in sharing this story that you will take a moment to create a forgiving moment, if one needs to be created in your life now or in the future. Here's my story. I once became upset at a great friend of mine, actually a childhood best friend. Now if you ask me what happened it really would not make sense. The misunderstanding was merely due to gossip and really had nothing to do with either of us. Regardless, the relationship became a nonexistent one. Months and months went by, no calls, no communication, silence. I was pregnant at the time of the miscommunication, I finally had the baby and I so wanted to share the joy of this moment with my friend, but I didn't. I remember the Holy Spirit tugging at me to pay her a visit, but I didn't budge, I made excuses as to why I couldn't go see about my friend. One day the void of our silence towards each other just stopped. I remember as if it was yesterday, It was early morning and I was sitting in the drive-thru line of Starbucks.

My phone rang, I answered joyfully and on the other end I heard a voice ask have you spoken to Lisa and I replied no I haven't. Is she sick? I responded. The next words that left the mouth of the person on the other end took my breath away. The person said Lisa was found in her bed this morning unresponsive. She's gone Ryan. Gone. No longer alive. What? This could not be real. I kept saying, no, no, no this is not happening. This moment could not be real. I was speechless after that, my heart was beyond heavy, and all I could think of was I never told my friend I was sorry or even said I forgive her. I lost my moment, my opportunity to let my friend know how much I loved her. See forgiveness would have freed me from this moment. So, I share that you won't make the same mistake I did. That you will forgive as quickly as you can and not walk around with the burden of unforgiveness, it's not worth it. If I could turn back the clock, I would. Life is too short to not forgive more.

Fear-Less Thoughts:

Do you currently have some forgiving to do?

_____
_____
_____
_____

When do you plan to free yourself and take the bold step to forgive?

_____
_____
_____
_____

List the benefits to forgiving.

_____
_____
_____
_____

What are the negative effects of not forgiving?

_____
_____
_____
_____

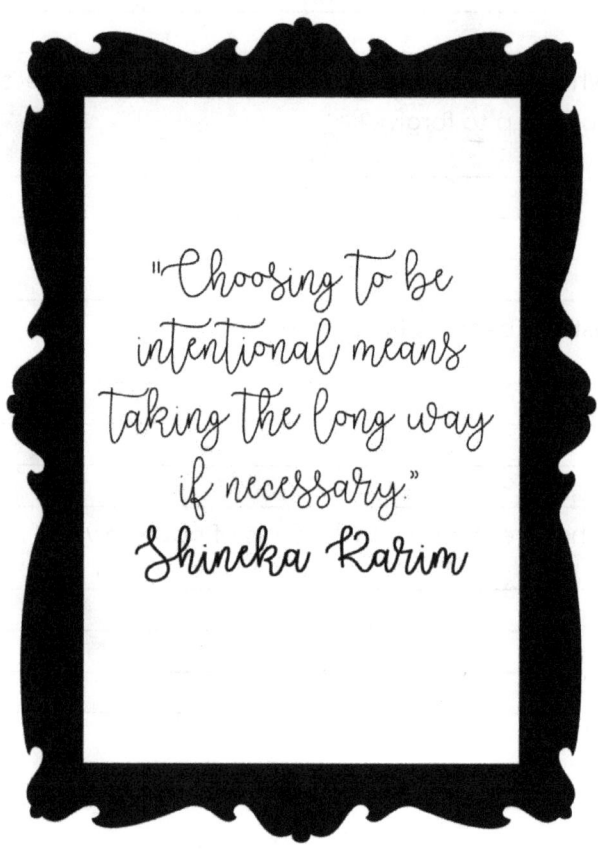

DAY 13: BE MORE INTENTIONAL

"Intentional action creates intentional results."
~Ryan Blair-Smith

The power in being more intentional is a game changer to creating the success you want to see in life, period. Intentional thinking leads to intentional strategizing slash planning, that leads into intentional action. The more you are intentional in your thought process, the better you are at controlling that stinkin' thinkin' that Joyce Meyer talks about. Stinkin' thinkin' is the enemy's way of getting you to self-sabotage yourself with negative self-talk, which eventually keeps you from achieving results in life. The power of intention is a crucial component that I truly want you to grab ahold of. Put a bookmark on this chapter, and remember that whatever you seek you must be intentional about obtaining. Taking time to focus on what you want comes from your intentional action. For instance, your weight loss happens when you intentionally think it is possible to achieve, when you intentionally plan out how you are going to create results, and then you intentionally take action with the steps you outlined for yourself. Let me tell you this, I did not lose 84 pounds by sitting on the couch. I lost the weight by being more intentional and fear-ing less of what I thought I could not do. I lost the weight because I intentionally got to the gym at 4:45 am daily for almost a year and killed it, in the gym. I lost the weight because I intentionally created a plan. I lost the weight because I intentionally took action. Truthfully we all have the gift, we all can be more intentional, it's not a gift that only one person has. Question is how are you going to use yours?

Fear-Less Thoughts:

How can you start being more intentional?

_____
_____
_____
_____

With what?

_____
_____
_____
_____

What have you done in the past that was intentional?

_____
_____
_____
_____

What effort did it take from you?

_____
_____
_____
_____

DAY 14: CONNECT MORE

"Connection is KEY"
~Jonathan Sprinkles

I definitely believe the quote by Mr. Sprinkles above is so true. Connection is KEY! May I add your connection with others should be valued as priceless. I think sometimes we may take our connection to others for granted, that we don't see the real value until the relationship has been broken or just sizzles away for lack of staying in touch. I heard something very profound shared by Mr. Sprinkles recently on one of his live radio broadcasts, he stated, "That in our pursuit to build empires in our business, that honestly our empires are built based on our relationships. Our connection to others." Think about it. Think about the genuine relationships you have with others in your circle who want you to succeed just as bad as you do. You win, they win and vice versa. Connections that are not just one-sided, but mutually beneficial striving to connect with like-minded individuals will definitely help you in connecting and creating relationships that last. I am sure you have heard that your circle of influence will determine how far you go, so choose wisely and prayerfully to those you connect with. Don't be fearful of networking and taking time to connect, it is more beneficial than you will ever know. I am not just saying that to you, I am sharing that with myself as well. This has been an area in my life that I want to grow and develop, because I know it's importance.

Fear-Less Thoughts:

How's your connection with others?

_____
_____
_____
_____

Do you think it is an area of opportunity or are you crushing it?

_____
_____
_____
_____

When's the last time you sent a letter to someone you are connected to?

_____
_____
_____
_____

It can be a thinking of you, a great job, or a let's connect soon. Who's in your circle?

_____
_____
_____
_____

Are you guys really helping each other reach the next level in your businesses and life?

_____
_____
_____
_____

DAY 15: TAKE MORE ACTION

"It's easy to dream about it, but much harder to execute it.....ACT NOW."
~Unknown

I hope you're fired up and ready to take some massive action right now. I pray you're starting to really see that fearing-less in life can truly open more doors of opportunity and free you of those things that may have previously trapped you. Taking action is the key, period!! The vision board I just challenged you to create in day eleven will not come to life without action. You can only pray for so long. At some point you must play your part; and know, your action is required. When you do decide to start taking action, don't wait on things to be perfect. Perfectionism is just the enemies attempt to sabotage you from creating the life you desire. Perfectionism creeps in like a thief in the night, without warning. Just take a step, then another step, then another step. Every step you take will start building up your confidence muscles as my coach, Coach Glitter always says. She is so right. Every step builds a momentum of mental strength and a "can do" attitude, and even if fear tries to creep in, you know, one action step is all you need to get started. If you stop here in this book and don't go any further, I want you to remember the simple truth of creating a life you want and love requires your action!

FEAR-LESS DO MORE

Fear-Less Thoughts:

You've created your vision board, you gotten a few tools to fear-less do more in life....what's next?

_____
_____
_____
_____

What action can you take right now in the direction of your dreams and goals?

_____
_____
_____
_____

List below what is standing in your way of taking action?

_____
_____
_____
_____

How can you overcome those distractions?

_____
_____
_____
_____

DAY 16: FAIL MORE

"Failure is the opportunity to begin again more intelligently."
~**Henry Ford**

Fear of failing is a real phobia that unfortunately haunts many on a daily basis. It traps individuals to never take action, because they are caught up in the notion of "what if" I fail. To the "what ifers," I say, "what if" you succeed. What if you walk away victorious and better than you started. I have struggled with the fear of failing and it has cost me many great opportunities in life. My good friend calls this loss in not taking action, "opportunity cost," and I agree. Opportunity cost is defined as the loss of potential gain from other alternatives when one alternative is chosen. In the failing scenario we are discussing now, most choose no action over fear of failing. To that I say, fail fast, fail now, and fail often. Know that your failure will produce more gains than losses in your life. Who cares if you fail? At least you took the time to try. Failing more will allow you to stretch yourself outside of your comfort zone. Failing more will allow you to start truly taking risks. Failing more will cause you to stop worrying and holding on to past failures. Failing more will ultimately aid you in learning from your mistakes. You will gain more clarity on what works and doesn't work well. You will gain more confidence. You will win in creating the action, you've dreaded taking action on. Michael Jordan said it best, *"I've failed over and over and over again in my life and that is why I succeed."* If we take time to look at a few successful people in history, it is evident that success takes work and failure is a part of it. We just have to remember the setbacks don't actually set us back, but set us up to succeed. Simply put we are failing forward. Here are a few successful people, I would like you to think about as it pertains to success and failure.

Let's start with the man of big dreams and dreaming out loud himself, Mr. Walt Disney. Of course you know how his story ends, magically indeed, but let me share a non-sparkly version of his journey. He was once told by his editor that he lacked imagination and had no good ideas.

Imagine his confidence level at this point and the fear of not being good enough to keep pushing in the industry. Can you imagine there not being a Mickey Mouse? Disney World? I am sorry I can't picture that life, but I'm glad he pushed forward. The second person I wanted to share with you is the Queen of TV herself, Oprah Winfrey. Oprah was fired from her first newscaster position. In the beginning of her career, she could have been crushed from this apparent failing moment, but she wasn't crushed, she took the failing moment to find what worked in her industry and excelled in it. Oprah has been noted as one of the richest women in the world and now has her own network, enough said. She exemplified failing forward at its finest. So to you, I say fear-less and fail more you never know how your story ends until you dare to try with action.

Fear-Less Thoughts:

When is the last time you failed at something?

_____
_____
_____
_____

What did you learn from the experience?

_____
_____
_____
_____

What are you going to do next time?

_____
_____
_____
_____

Research other successful people that have failed and list at least three below. What did you learn from them sharing their failure?

_____
_____
_____
_____
_____
_____
_____
_____
_____

"Open your mouth. Declare your desire. And watch God open doors, windows, and garages for you."
JeNae Clark

DAY 17: TRUST GOD MORE

"Trust in the Lord with all your heart, and do not lean on your own understanding. In all your ways acknowledge him, and He will make straight your paths."
~Proverbs 3:5-6

When it comes to living, thinking, dreaming and operating in our gifts, trusting God is the biggest thing we can do in life period. If we take more time to fear-less and trust God more in our journey, we will live a more fulfilled and joyous life. A life that is free of worry and daily stresses. I am convinced that all those times I didn't take time to trust God in the process, dragged on longer than they should have. I sabotaged myself by thinking I was in control of my situation, and really I was extremely out of control in it. I think Joyce Meyer states it best on how we should think and speak to moments of not trusting God as we should, she gives this challenge, to say this out loud. "The Lord is going to take care of this. It doesn't matter what it looks like—I believe God is working!"

I challenge you to repeat that statement out loud. Lastly, there are three things that I would like to leave on your heart from this lesson:

1. We must trust more in God and less in ourselves. Regardless of how in control we think we are.
2. Worrying less will leave less stress on your mental and physical being.
3. Know that God is steps beyond where you see the situation. He is just waiting on you to seek him in the process.

Fear-Less Thoughts:

Think about a time when you could have trusted God more.

_____
_____
_____
_____

What did you learn?

_____
_____
_____
_____

How do plan on trusting God more going forward?

_____
_____
_____
_____

FEAR-LESS DO MORE

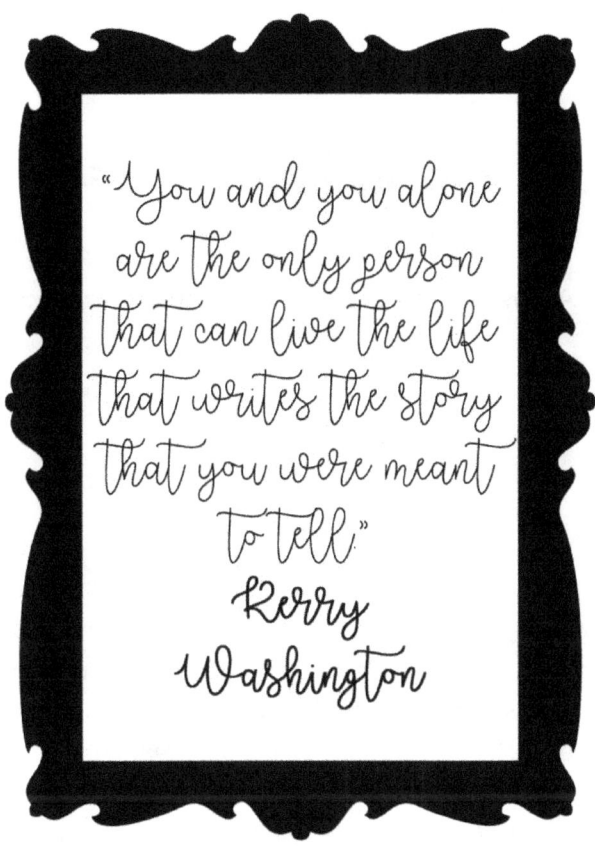

"You and you alone are the only person that can live the life that writes the story that you were meant to tell."
Kerry Washington

DAY 18: FOCUS MORE

"Always remember your focus determines your reality."
~George Lucas

I get it. Focusing on major projects, small daily tasks, and life can seem hard to do. Especially if you are being pulled in 101 different directions. As a mom, my job or passion project of love is to pour love, wisdom, and strength into my daughters. It takes energy and skills. I also wear many hats beyond my mommy role and when all the different roles that I walk in start tugging, I sometimes lose my focus and get sidetracked. Now I am not using motherhood or wifely duties as an excuse. What I am identifying is that "roles" can have you unfocused or you can use them as an excuse because of fear. So for me as an example. I have made a thousand excuses why I cannot sit my butt down to write a book. The truth was, there was a little fear there. What if people don't buy the book, what if people don't care period. I was wrapped up in what-ifs and coulda, woulda, shouldas, that I kept pushing myself further away from my goal of publishing my own book. If you are reading this book, that means I traded in my fears for focus. I dared myself to do more with my time and use it wisely. I decided to go after my dream and focus on what I really wanted. I challenge you to let go of the excuses that block your focus. Focus is key to your success. Trust me!

Fear-Less Thoughts:

On a scale of 1 to 10 (10 being the high end) what is your level of focus right now?

_____
_____
_____
_____

If you scored lower in the category of focus, how do you plan on fixing this slight roadblock?

_____
_____
_____
_____

What do you want to focus more on?

_____
_____
_____
_____

And how do you plan on focusing more? Remember having a game plan is key to overcoming the lack of focus.

_____
_____
_____
_____
_____
_____
_____
_____

"I sow where I would like to grow."
Toni Ellis

DAY 19: GROW MORE

*"The more that you read,
The more things you will know,
The more that you LEARN,
The more places you'll go."*
~**Dr. Seuss**

I was laughing with a friend about her life-time learner mindset. She recently enrolled in a course to get her masters. She is a busy mom of three amazing little boys, one of them is new to the world. Baby mode is part of the mix, she is an entrepreneur, works for a company, and the list goes on. Her love for learning has never sizzled and I commend her passion for continually striving to grow. Truthfully, we all have opportunity to continually grow and develop. I don't think we are ever too young, too old, or simply too busy to strive for more. I think it is key to your success to continually develop in various, maybe even all areas of your life. Don't ever think you have it all figured out. Challenge yourself to take your business to another level, your parenting skills to another level, your marriage to another level, your current level of knowledge to another level by seeking more knowledge. Your growth can come from reading more, taking classes, joining a coaching program, or finding a mentor to glean from. Don't let fear of thinking you don't have enough, or you're too old, or it will be too hard to learn, or any other sabotaging thoughts that are keeping you from taking that bold leap to grow more. I promise you will surprise yourself in what you can accomplish by taking the time to expand your knowledge, as Dr. Seuss says in the quote above, "The more that you learn, the more places you'll go."

Fear-Less Thoughts:

What do you plan on doing in the next 21 days that will help you grow?

_____
_____
_____
_____

What books are you reading that will help you in your business, job, or life?

_____
_____
_____
_____

Ask others what books they suggest, if you're not sure where to start?

_____
_____
_____
_____

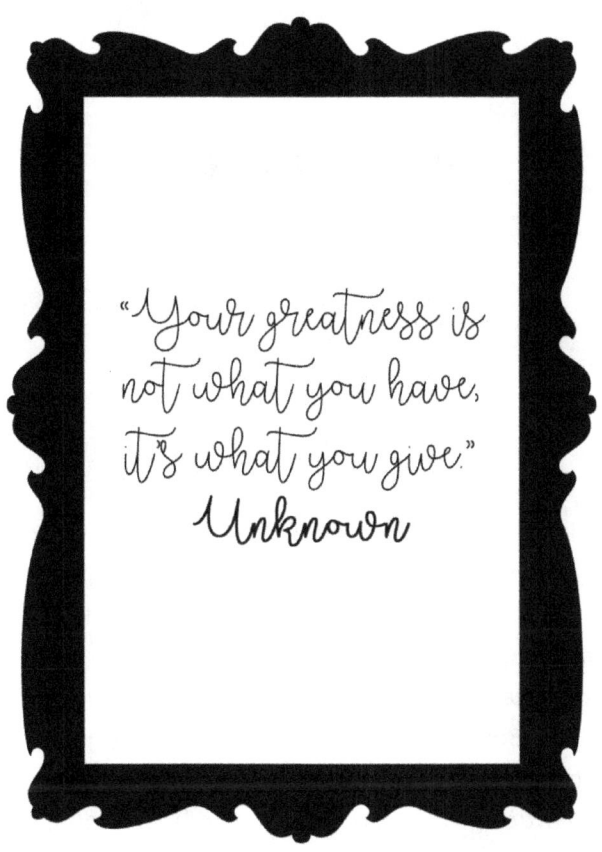

DAY 20: GIVE MORE

*"We make a living by what we get, but
We make a LIFE by what we give."*
~Winston Churchill

I absolutely love the quote for this chapter by Winston Churchill, please let me repeat it back to you. "We make a living by what we get, but we make a life by what we give." This is the mother of all quotes to me. I believe it sums up our mission in life. Being of service to others, sharing our gifts and talents, giving of our time to those in need. The art of giving comes from the heart and cannot be valued by any dollar amount. Giving is definitely a heart matter, the core is love. Giving has a way of changing your entire perspective about life in general. To be honest there are so many ways to give, it does not have to be money. It can be giving of your time, talent, and a listening ear. Like I mentioned above it does not require much, just as long as it is coming from the heart. The Bible says it best of course in Deuteronomy 15:10, *"Give generously to them and do so without a grudging heart; then because of this the Lord your God will bless you in all your work and in everything you put your hands to."* It says give generously and not grudgingly. If I ever feel as though I am giving grudgingly, I simply will not do it. I promise giving from the heart feels a whole lot better in the end. Sometimes in giving, people will fear what they will lose in the process versus what they would gain and that is so unfortunate. I dare you to fear-less in giving, and go all in from the heart, and give more.

Fear-Less Thoughts:

When is the last time you gave?

_____
_____
_____
_____

How did you feel afterwards?

_____
_____
_____
_____

Are there any organizations that align with your core values that you could start supporting?

_____
_____
_____
_____

DAY 21: LOVE MORE

"And now these three remain faith, hope, love. But the greatest of these is love."
~1 Corinthians 13:13

I am super excited to end our last day together with the focus on loving more! I cannot thank God enough for giving me the vision to conclude with this chapter. I also want to say thank you and I love you for joining me on this 21-day journey. I pray that you were blessed and walked away with some rich nuggets on how to Fear-Less and Do More in your life's journey.

Since I still have your attention. Can I tell you what I think of love? I believe love conquers all. I believe love is the core of our being. I believe love overlooks hurt and can heal wounds. I believe love can set you free. I believe love is the key ingredient that can take an ordinary life to an extraordinary one! I believe what the Bible says about love, it is the greatest out of faith, hope, and love. I believe it is your time to fear-less and love your life, your relationships, your dreams, your journey, and all that you have been called to be. Life is way too short to hate the cards you were dealt, or worry about what's not happening in the order you thought it should. I challenge to love wherever you are in life, embrace it, rock it, learn from it, and simply find joy in it. I would hate for you to miss out on life, because you have not decided to love in the moment.

Fear-Less Thoughts:

What do you love about your life?

_____
_____
_____
_____

What do you love about your job, family, career, or spouse?

_____
_____
_____
_____

What do you need to embrace more of and fear-less about?

_____
_____
_____
_____

Day One Date: _____

Five things I am GRATEFUL for:

"I will strive to be a better person I was the day before, and I will always have sincere faith."
-Stephanie Davis

FEAR-LESS DO MORE

Day Two   Date: _____

Five things I am GRATEFUL for:

"I refuse to be a passenger in my own life."
-Crystal Layland

Day Three   Date: _____

Five things I am GRATEFUL for:

"Your message is not for you. It is for the people who literally need you to save their lives and change the trajectory of their future."
-JeNae Clark

Day Four   Date: _____

Five things I am GRATEFUL for:

"Only what I do for CHRIST will last!"
-Artisha Harris-Woody

Day Five   Date: _____

Five things I am GRATEFUL for:

"Stop chasing the money. Chase your purpose and the money will run you over."
-Martha Cooper Hudson

FEAR-LESS DO MORE

Day Six   Date: _____

Five things I am GRATEFUL for:

""The rain may get heavy and the winds blow hard but my God is greater than it all! I may get wet but I am still covered."
~C. Marie

Day Seven   Date: _____

Five things I am GRATEFUL for:

"Faith trumps fear."
-Blondy Moore

FEAR-LESS DO MORE

Day Eight   Date: _____

Five things I am GRATEFUL for:

"My past does not define me. I am not what happened to me. I am what I choose to become."
-Jennifer Fontanilla

Day Nine   Date: _____

Five things I am GRATEFUL for:

""I'm not perfect but I'm still a privilege."
-Alfreda Benford

FEAR-LESS DO MORE

Day Ten						Date: _____

Five things I am GRATEFUL for:

*"There is something perfect about everyone's reflection
that kindles love esteem in others.
Embrace your sparkle."*
-Toni Ellis

Day Eleven Date: _____

Five things I am GRATEFUL for:

*Confidence is my vehicle and
I'm driving it all the way to success!*
-Leslie Lester

FEAR-LESS DO MORE

Day Twelve   Date: _____

Five things I am GRATEFUL for:

"Your purpose is greater than your struggle."
-Andrena Philips

Day Thirteen   Date: _____

Five things I am GRATEFUL for:

*"One thing which has the ability to limit your greatness
is the inability to recognize your power."*
-Shineka Karim

FEAR-LESS DO MORE

Day Fourteen					Date: _____

Five things I am GRATEFUL for:

"I wasn't created to fit into anyone's mold. In order for my greatness to impact the world the way that it will; life had to happen for me the way that it did! No excuses allowed."
-Rasheena Perry

Day Fifteen   Date: _____

Five things I am GRATEFUL for:

"I sow where I would like to GROW."
-Toni Ellis

FEAR-LESS DO MORE

Day Sixteen					Date: _____

Five things I am GRATEFUL for:

"Let gratitude be the pillow upon which you kneel to say your nightly prayer."
-Dr. Maya Angelou

Day Seventeen   Date: _____

Five things I am GRATEFUL for:

"God needs your availability not visibility. Your aim should be to serve and not to be seen." #LevelUp
-Melody Joy

FEAR-LESS DO MORE

Day Eighteen   Date: _____

Five things I am GRATEFUL for:

""Goals serve as a checks and balance system for what you promised to do long before doubt or distractions showed up."
-Shineka Karim

Day Nineteen   Date: _____

Five things I am GRATEFUL for:

"Open your mouth, declare your desire and watch God open doors, windows and garages for you."
-JeNae Clark

FEAR-LESS DO MORE

Day Twenty   Date: _____

Five things I am GRATEFUL for:

"Choosing to be intentional means taking the long way if necessary."
-Shineka Karim

Day Twenty One   Date: _____

Five things I am GRATEFUL for:

"The Birthing Process consists of, Pain which produces Pressure, Pressure which produces Power, and Power which provokes you to Push! Don't you dare abort that baby, breathe in and give it another PUSH!
         -Rasheena Perry

FEAR-LESS DO MORE

NOTES

RYAN BLAIR-SMITH

NOTES

www.ingramcontent.com/pod-product-compliance
Lightning Source LLC
Chambersburg PA
CBHW071138090426
42736CB00012B/2149